BALEFIRE

POETRY FOR THE END OF THE WORLD

ELIZABETH WILDER

CONTENTS

AN INTRODUCTION, OF SORTS

balefire, n.
  \ ˈbāl-ˌfī(-ə)r \

1. a large, outdoor fire; a bonfire.
2. the fire associated with a funeral pyre.
3. a signal fire; a beacon.

I

SPARK

I ask god who

I am

    meant

               to be

   and

god does not

             answer

                    back

- freedom [to fail]

my mother called me a witch
because she was afraid
to say *bitch*. my father said
I could be anything but closed
his eyes to this cracked heart.
my grandmother said I should
visit Italy out of fealty to the family
that hurt me. the man
I gave my first kiss said without
speaking that he wanted a body
without a mind, and the church
made me want a mind without
a body. my husband said nothing.

so many names and rules and faces
to wear, and none of them suit.

I am tired of trying
to figure
out who
I am meant
to be —

- nearly forty years old

she bleeds, she births,
she cuts her soft heart
from her chest and feeds
it to her sons, praying
the offering will grow
them into men with soft
hearts and clear minds and
kind hands, knowing
the world will
hate them for it.

- motherhood & misogyny

"scripture"

The ancient texts have nothing
that shows
how and who a woman can be
except:

    silent
    suffering
    child-bearer
    victim
    villain —

how small-
minded to think a god
who created universes could suffer
such a lack
of imagination —

my experience of my own
motherhood is as one
unending groan
for help that never comes.

I am so tired of fighting
tooth and claw while
everyone I see seems
to float, uncaring, through
these turning days —

- admitting defeat is relief
/ let someone else do the caring

asking the right questions
  / building a new table

sixteen years old and I was writing
Lines about Mary's bloody birth
in a filth stable, wondering if she
and me and the female we, with blood
between our thighs, were too
much —

   now I realize
   we are just
   what the church
   of men is in
   need of —

I am turquoise turned indigo with
the blood
let by my soul.
I am square longing
to be circle.
I skip with a hopeful limp.

I am a whimper building
to a searing roar.
I am a deer, ordinary
as a fairy.
I am the song of the unicorn
forgotten by the ark.
I am fourfold.

I am a chair tired
of being sat on.

if only more men
could re-

　　member

the skin
they wear
was knit
by woman's blood and
bone, born
of her power and her
yielding, that she —

　　we —

could have dug them from
our wombs, and didn't —
maybe they would stop

　　hurting us

　　　　　then.

　　　　　　　　- the patriarchy's deepest shame

honey is sweeter than blood,
you say as if I should know
what the hell that means, as
if you are expressing the sentiment
of love, as if we aren't living
on the west side of
the isle of the dead. you strip

your clothes off like a goddess
snake being reborn, shedding
its latest immortal cells,
as if you are Kali and I am your
temple slave, ardent with sub-
servient, iron-clad passion. but
I am merely a cathedral of thumbs,
a soft monster with eyes only for

escape. you show me
your breasts as if they are more
than physical while I play
the invisible harp of our
disembodied end. honey

is sweeter than blood, I'll say
as if it means something, as if
it is anything more than
my break for freedom.

how long
until my sons
learn to be
ashamed of their
mother because
she is
a woman
?

- motherhood ancient & modern

I played by their
rules my whole damn life —

    dutiful daughter
    dutiful wife
    dutiful mother —

a world of men
still screaming
I've got it all wrong.

    so I called

that bluff

    and walked

                        away.

    surprise, surprise
    only then did I find

truth

    freedom

                    myself —

                            - the game

I am a blue tree in a crimson
forest where nobody bleeds
(they say) and the plants smile
at the fall as if it is not the beginning
of their end, and I don't

understand why they die so quietly,
like they don't know they are
passing, leaves wilting, falling for
the last time. I am

a blue tree in a crimson forest,
but I gather up my roots and wander
to where I am a blue tree in a
blue forest, where the loam feels
like home and the wide rainbow
stretches wild as a weed.

true love does
not demand
a sacrifice.

it is difficult
to understand how
some can believe the pain
they create
is right.

- justified by an ugly end

I let
the tears fall,
having long
forgotten what
they are for.

my daughter's ninth birthday / stillbirth

it is my daughter's
ninth
birthday and I
do not know
what to get
her because
she is
still
dead.

breathe.
breathe.
breathe.
breathe.
breathe.

- this panic attack will pass in
fifteen to thirty minutes

a forest fire is a rescue
effort, a cleansing and renewal
of the ever-giving earth.

when the world goes up
in flame every summer, it is
the earth herself
screaming, pleading for us to give
her rest.

- what will it take for us to listen

autumn

trees afire
with raucous
color, daring the biting
air to pluck their leaves
from the bluest sky —

    the world changes,
    turns, transforms with
    reckless joy.

so
can
I
?

the questions
are
the answer

II

SMOLDER

new year, same year

the skeleton of who
I once was sits up
in her coffin and asks why
I'm still
not using this body
to dance wild in the broken
and wild streets, summoning
the cadence of hope back
to hearts gone
arid too long —

it is a terrible thing
to be a soft-spun man
in a world of teeth

- the patriarchy

we are a nation starving

    for silence

                safety

                            song.

they say: write
what you hear, what
you know. I hear
the rage
of the trees,
the quiet
of needed voices
going silent. I hear
my doubt
my fear
my zeal to make
this short string
of days matter, my limping
frustration that I cannot
fucking seem to.
my children grow
old before my eyes but what
have I done? we've given
them a fractured
world nearly
beyond
repair.

I used to think
I'd be
happier living
in another time with fuller
skirts and tighter
corsets, but

having lived
longer in this one, I know
better
now.

- the world has always hated "difficult" women

I am your one earth, your only home.

You shall tend me as gently as you nurture a child.

You shall see my worth, and yours, beyond what can be taken from us.

Keep wild these lands and the tribes who hold them as holy.

Honor the bodies that gave you life, but do not hold yourself in bondage to them.

Honor all life.

Honor all love.

Mark health boundaries.

Honor all truth.

Open your hands. Share your surplus with those who need.

Abandon fear. Pursue learning. Hold tight to common sense.

Follow these laws, my child, and you and all people shall be forever blessed.

is a mother's love enough
to grow beautifully feral
boys into kind and caring men?

- [I fear it is not]

when will I learn
to stop fighting this heart-
broken body when she
cries out

for water
for gentleness
for rest
?

the heartbreaking hope inherent
in a single
wild
daisy opening brave
petals to the forever sky.

- climate change unchecked

what gall or madness must it require
to sit before a nation, a world
of aching hearts that know the truth

                                        and lie?

ancestry

humanity is a deep well
of darkness. when you drink
from it, you never know
if you will receive water or
a mouthful of daggers.

when will the world stop
spinning for the few and lay
itself back in the care of the ancients,
the indigenous, the wild, the only
ones who ever knew
how to love her well
anyway?

- the curse of the white male

we are
destroying the only
home
we have
ever known.

- climate change

the positive pregnancy test.
her first kicks felt.
fresh-washed baby clothes.
the belief that I am a mother.

your kisses on my shivering neck.

his infant giggle.
first steps.
first words.

the earth solid beneath my soles.
the flaming hope of each new sun.

the solace of your arms around me.

all
at
once
the world was too small

    — no space left to be alone and free and safe outside
                your home that shrinks every damn day

and too big

    — to cure, to coerce to kindness, to care about each
                    other or ourselves

we are the problem
[un?]fortunately, we are
also the answer.

- pandemic

altar

I built a shrine to
our obsolescence, thinking
it would be our rescue
vessel in the fracturing
storm we created, but

it listed in the bleak
water like a starry-eyed
fool drunk on dreams
and festering hope, filling
with sea-depths and stories
from five fathoms down
in the black and grueling fantasy
we built on disintegrating kisses.
the sacred wood is dank
with rotten ardor and
unsaid words, with uneaten
communion and half-burned
incense gone
cold as a star.

Grandma
(I don't even know your middle name)

the world went on
without you, as you knew
it would. but
I think of you more
than ever —

if the PTSD your husband back from World War II with
had a name, if he hit you, if you loved him anyway —

how you weathered the corsets of your girlhood on
through famines and wars and all this damned tech-
nology and how you never lost yourself —

how you sold pasta in Brooklyn and stillbirthed a baby
just like me, and if you got to hold that aunt I never
knew, if you thought of her often as you fed sheets of
uncut spaghetti through the machine that sliced it to
pieces —

or if you never really knew who you were, and if that's
why the last time we met you ate onion crisps and crin-
kled your eyes at me and said you needed to eat them
to fill the void —

how could you leave
before I knew how
much I needed
you, before I learned
how you kept on

breathing through
the dark —

fuck the patriarchy

daughters, the world hates women

who speak strong
who smile too much (but not enough)
who don't ask permission —

    come, let us be
    such women anyway.

sunlight on snow is
too loud for my eyes
and too bright for my ears.

- sensory processing disorder

I'm tired of swallowing

    every morning I glare
    at these pills and wonder
    if I'll ever live
    without them. I hate

        and love

    them.
    Everyday they save
    me. Everyday I swallow them with
    a ghost
    of hope
    that one day I can leave

        them

            forever.

- mental health meds
/ the lies we tell ourselves about our life-saving medications

we move through
the world as if these
bodies were more
than flesh, as if we were
more than one
breathless moment away
from destruction, as if some
hours mattered less or more
than others, as if death
was forever deferred,
as if we have time
to waste, as if half or more
of humanity didn't exist
on next next to nothing,
as if every breath was not
sacred, every exhalation
practice for the inevitable

last.

does love still
conquer all these
days? or have we
commodified that
too?

- *late stage capitalism*

justice may not have found
its way to your deserving doorstep

yet.

this does not mean
your actions

are right.

- the white male privilege of the benefit of the doubt
/ me too

too much

                           not enough

too much

                           not enough

- I refuse to dance within the li[n]es you have drawn for us

if you must turn hard
to survive, don't
let it be against

yourself.

the day you find yourself
empty is the day you can
truly begin.

- when all the tears are shed

III

BURN

we are an earthquake
daring you
to ignore our
shuddering portents —

    watch us tear
    this earth open
    and devour your
    rapacious deeds.

    our children
    will play in the dust
    of your undoing.

- the breaking point of the unheard
/ enough is enough

you say
I am
a pebble in your
shoe like that's a bad thing.

I say
look
how I made you take
heed of my presence and power.

- write your representatives

anger is the sorrow
you never allowed
yourself to feel.

to the patriarchy:

all my life —
woman,
women,
this woman:
labelled
too much and
not enough.

it took four decades but
I finally see why
you lie —

    you fear the
    our velvet power, knowing
    the trades you've forced down
    our throats are not,
    never will be, enough.

    you have lied so long, you've forgotten
    what truth tastes like.

    do not fear — we are
    waking and sampling all
    that you kept
    from us.

I hope to see
you weep
for what you have wrought.

love that you need
to beg for
is not real
love

lies I've swallowed

I walked into my womb
and found a room filled
with razors that
taught me to hate
myself, my body, my voice —

I gather them into
my hands and let
myself bleed, weeping
for all the wasted time —

    and then I light
    a fire right
    there in my belly
    and burn
    it all until the old
    metal is melted and turned
    new — a coat

    of armor, intuition I
    willingly wear, a testament
    to the resilience
    you almost made
    me forget
    I possess —

air to breathe
water to drink
walls to call home
work that sustains
love to share

- a life of liberty prone to happiness
/ inalienable rights

when
will I be finished
fighting this war

with
my
body?

I beg the moon to tell
me who
I am, who
I'm meant
to be. she never
speaks because how
can she hold
secrets that live
inside me?

- learning to listen

I toss glances at those who have a god
and my lashes drip with envy. so
sure, so safe, they think, and I

am left sinking into mystery,
alternately glorious and grotesque,
this bag of blood-salted questions.

my seeking is overripe, over-
done, so I feast on this lack
of answers, juice dripping down

my chin, and I am nourished. I
feel my bones grow whole again,
muscles reforming, and breathe fresh

fire instead of fervor while the flies
dawdle by on their way to the rotten,
mealy carcass called certainty.

we fear the wind and the night
because we know one day that same
breeze will lift us away
into the forever

dark.

the ancient amber
light of sunset reminds
me that, no matter
what humanity
does with itself, the earth
will go on beyond us.

    this is a strange
    comfort that warms
    my throat and threadbare

            brain.

wells cathedral

I'd stopped believing
the church of men had anything
but poison to offer my full-
breasted body and blood and
fathomless brain. but beneath

the sunlit medieval stones
the priest remembered to pray
for minds that flirt with fear too
long, too often, and the organ
music began and I drank
it in through the tired

soles of my feet, toes spreading
like the thirsty roots of a sun-
blanched rose that barely recalls
how to bloom and I wonder

> if there isn't a god
> for me
> everywhere
> after all

the labyrinth

spiral stones and paths
to wander, grass fields
spilling lush up to jagged
mountains' feet, bees
that sing and birds that buzz
above the lavender buds — here

    my heart feels
    wild and free and,
    settling, breathes

                again.

when was the last time you allowed
yourself to listen
to the wind?
ancient as dirt, witness
to eternity. has it brushed
the cheek of every human
who ever breathed? I like to imagine

it has.

don't talk
to yourself
the way
they did.

- verbal abuse

they say he is too wild and loud and electric
as a summer storm tumbling in, tripping
over its own thunderous feet, overflowing
with inconvenient delight to share
its finger-slicked painting
of light and sound. i say

he doesn't need
to be stopped, squashed,
only channeled.

his offering is honest and more
than a little dirt-stained. this is his
freedom, his gift and his power.

can't you see? it was ours
once,
too.

my fat cat, black
and sleek, never
doubts she is
goddess made
flesh while I
fail to believe it for
myself in a thousand
different moments
every day.

Forget about "being good at."
Abandon society's demand for mastery.
Leave it on the side of the road at your earliest convenience.

Let it rot.

Let the vultures wheel above its petrifying carcass. Let it unfold the molecules of its being and release them back to the earth to be cleansed, healed, used as fodder for life that is real.

Refuse to host its festering presence in the perfect imperfection of your humanity, lest it devour your soul from the inside out.

Unburden thyself.

Abandon these needless shackles.

Love the work you choose, and allow its glorious flaws. Throw your whole body and being into sweet amateurity.

Taste, maker, and be free.

a rich man blinks and makes
a million that he'd never miss
if he used it to help the world back
to its feet. so how has he

convinced the rest of us
to blame each other that all
our work is never, ever,
ever enough to keep our heads
above the dark and devouring water?

- the "moral" minority

empathy
will save
the world, if we
ever
let it.

- bound and gagged

the lie of the west

I have no desire to play
the game set for us all —

> competition for what
> capitalism says there is not
> enough of while the very few
> each claim more
> than what the rest of us
> have all together.

I do not wish to play
a game rigged
to make losers of us all.

one hundred generations
stolen, robbed
of the history they could have,
would have
without our ships and
whips and auction blocks,
and still we say
we owe them
nothing —

- the hill we [make them] climb

Thanksgiving 2020

You taught us America
was the great
melting pot, then
fainted when we believed.

This is our dream, the one you birthed —

One nation made
of all nations, united
in love,
in justice,
in empathy and needed
reparations.

Give us the dream.

IV

BLAZE

I did not know
how to love you
because I did not
know how to love
myself.

the girl I couldn't cherish
becomes the women I will die
as, and

these heavy eyes are my
grandmother's, stubborn and
elegant — these aches are the rent
I willingly pay for another year beneath
the sun — the lines in my flesh testify to
the joy and pain that have made me
into this person who is so
unexpectedly alive.

I am the love of my life.

The taste of hope long deferred
is sweet, yet unfamiliar.
Palates have grown used
to sorrow, betrayal, pain. Can
the hurting relearn
to trust the honey long denied?

- January 20, 2021

summer thunder tumbling
from dark mountains of cloud tears
an opening
in the wall
I've built
between
myself
and
mySelf.
my throat cracks wide, my heart
trembles, my chin tips back and I
weep with relief
in rhythm
with the
rain.

to the artists, november 2016

pen to paper, brush
to paint, this is how
we live — by
beauty and color, velvet night
and star-spangled day. this

is how we we live —
by fiery transmutation
of our everydays, by
seeing the eternal
in the ordinary, the
universe in a single fallen
skin cell. we press our hands
toward our art so we may share
these rainbowed riches with
a world starved. this is

how we live, how we reclaim
our selves.

keep going.

I come from the ancient
isle of women, hearts full as apples,
with bared feet and minds ripe
with questions dancing within
the sacred orchard.

I write like it matters.

if it does, I hope
I find out
before I die.

the doors are wide – climb
on board now. just begin. just
begin. just *begin,* for ideas are not
so scarce and somber that you must hoard
your hours and your terror for the ravenous
day when (you fear) all your syllables
are spent. begin, here,
there, the train is
passing always, pausing,
hoping open just for
you. just
begin. silver
grit, untamed
sparks sing
you to the rails.
begin.

pen to paper
foot to earth
eyes to sky
hand in hand in hand in hand
we go with
open hearts, undeterred
words crying
for liberty
for justice
for all
for all
for all
for all

- we pledge allegiance to each other
/ how we all rise

the scent of incense never
fails to make me
believe I existed before
my first cell came
to pulsing life —

feathers on a page
fallen like ancient
runes, as if I know
what they mean, as
if they are meant
for anyone but
the birds who shed
them
(I read the odd
symbology anyway
and find my whole
world rising up
to meet me)

there is not much I trust
so wholeheartedly as the musty-
scented pages of a book.

words are like water, washing
and washing us with their truth --
or otherwise drowning
us if we won't allow it, healing turned
to windswept tumult to get our
ever-wandering attention. they are

everywhere, reach everywhere, patient
enough to hollow out caverns
in the deep, strong enough to
tumble down the thin and ruinous
beliefs we clutch the closest. in
time, with ruthless endurance,

everything they touch transforms.

when the sky
is falling all
around you, don't
forget to see
what lives

beyond

all these broken pieces.

duality

our souls sip stardust
and holy fire and feast
on silver moon crust while
our soles crush each other's
porcelain hearts and trample
what is good and green and living.

there is nothing extraordinary

about you and me. we are gods
of blood and breath and bone,
birthed of painted paradox.
we are all the same, all
perfectly, imperfectly unique.

our love is a psalm, our fears
a festering wound. we are
nothing. we are
everything.
we are

everything can be used.

- a hopeful threat

the injury

the time I stretched
my calf muscle too thin and seemed to
snap like a brittle rubber band,
but didn't —

    a staring, the blue-scrubbed doctor
    with the bare scalp and dancing
    eyes said —

I'd been working
this body in the dim
garage to the cold gleam of an exercise
video chirping from my phone,
my knees stabbing
high toward the sky, toes pointed
to concrete earth, sweating like my body
isn't good enough, that all
its mitochondrial transformations mean
nothing, like this body isn't
in constant death
and resurrection, like it hasn't done enough
when really
it's done everything —

    of course it broke beneath
    the flail of my unabating hatred
    of it, begging for rest
    for peace, for
    love.

for the first time in my whole damn life,

I give my body everything
it's always wanted and never had. for
the first time, I allow
this skin and blood and bone
and sinew to become

a soft home

I feel grateful to live in.

the world says
the crow
is trash

a pest

a scavenger

but have you ever seen
so many colors
as in the velvet iridescence
of its proud feathers?

the cloud will pass
justice will prevail
the sun shall shine warm
and clear and bright on every
face because we did not stop until
we made the world that all people deserve.

- the riot of creation

you don't always need
to give. you don't always have
to be of service.
you are allowed
to simply
be

- a sigh of relief
/ this is more than enough

stretch your fingers toward
the sun, break
off a piece of cool blue
sky. put it in
your mouth and feel
it dissolve like sugar. take
a breath and feel
how your ribs shy
away from each
other, how good it is
for the flesh between
to thin just for
a moment like fresh
elastic. dig

your toes down, claw
up damp earth like ten
tiny backhoes. inhale.
savor the scent of fertile
ground as it fills
your caverns. remember
this, remember now —
tuck it away behind
your heart for when
you feel broken beyond

repair and your cheeks
are chapped with dried-
up tears — there is

always more
light, more ease, more
possibility waiting
for you at the hobbling
end of the bitterest
winter. look around
you and believe.

- spring
/ hope is a renewable resource

the gift of being

you ache to work and give,
to heal and serve, but remember

your existence is
about more than helping (although
that is good and needed) —

  you are also here to
  simply
  be.
  to breathe
  and laugh
  and learn
  and love.

                          live, but give to
                  yourSelf as well. give
                      your Self the gift
                          of being.

you would not strike
a match and set it out
in a windstorm —

do not demand
your single, nebulous
flame of love act
like a raging
bonfire before it
is ready —

- protect your treasure
/ boundaries

a day need not
be bright and warm
to be beautiful, and
neither

do

you

the bad news is
you cannot force someone to
love you.

the good news is
you
do not need
those who cannot
love you.

how could you ever be
a mistake? look
how many miracles
it took to make you.

I unlocked my body and it was a mystery
how I breathed bound for so damn long.
And now I live

with fear extracted like a rotten tooth.
I live for something, not in spite
of everything. I live like a dream built
on solid stone, a fortress
of soul and bone. I live like death
is a spark, not a curse. I live

with electric fire in my blood, ordinary
routine charged with meaning.
I live —

I can — I will — I am,
now, and

                now, and

                                now, and

ALSO BY ELIZABETH WILDER

Night Cycles is a lyrical collection of poems about life's deepest questions & brightest moments, all spun out under the wandering moon. Do you dare to step into the vulnerable black whose name is your own?

Available now in print and ebook.

A FREE EBOOK FOR YOU

CAN'T GET ENOUGH WILD(ER) WRITING?

Download *Odd Little Experiments,* a collection of four pastiches by
Elizabeth Wilder — totally free!

Get your free ebook: https://tinyurl.com/odd-wilder

ABOUT THE AUTHOR

Elizabeth Wilder writes, paints, and dreams in Montana. She is the author of the mystic poetry collection *Night Cycles*. Her words and art have appeared in various publications, such as xoJane, Somerset Studio, Still Standing Magazine, Wild Goslings, and Disney's Family Fun.

In addition to her quirky little family and their too-many naughty — and very much loved — dogs and cats, Elizabeth is in love with moon-gazing, dancing wild, and drinking too much coffee.

www.sheofthewild.com

amazon.com/Elizabeth-Wilder

instagram.com/sheofthewild

facebook.com/sheofthewild

twitter.com/sheofthewild

bookbub.com/authors/elizabeth-wilder